THE **MERCY FO**

# BEYOND

# STARVED

*Mercy for Eating Disorders*

*REAL STORIES* OF
*REAL FREEDOM*
WITH BONUS STUDY GUIDE

# NANCY ALCORN

WINEPRESS **WP** PUBLISHING

WinePress Publishing (PO Box 428, Enumclaw, WA 98022) functions only as book publisher. As such, the ultimate design, content, editorial accuracy, and views expressed or implied in this work are those of the author.

Unless otherwise noted, all Scriptures are taken from the *Holy Bible, New International Version®, NIV®.* Copyright © 1973, 1978, 1984 by the International Bible Society. Used by permission of Zondervan. All rights reserved.

ISBN 13: 978-1-57921-936-9
ISBN 10: 1-57921-936-5
Library of Congress Catalog Card Number: 2007937889

*To those who are* **desperate** *for help*
*But feel there is no hope,*
*This book has been placed in your* **hands** *for a reason—*
*It is no accident that you are reading this even now.*
*My* **prayer** *is that you will read on,*
*Because this book was written for you.*
*If you receive this message,*
*You will* **never** *be the same!*

—Nancy Alcorn

# CONTENTS

# INTRODUCTION

*A*fter reading *Starved: Mercy for Eating Disorders*, you should have a better understanding of what an eating disorder is and realize that through Christ, you can break free and stay free from this life-controlling issue.

Although it may seem innocent in the beginning, an eating disorder can quickly spiral out of control, leaving you feeling hopeless and alone. As you read this book, know that you are not alone in your struggle. Each chapter includes a story of a young woman who was once in bondage to an eating disorder, but as she applied the truth of God's Word to her life, she was transformed from the inside out. Read as each girl tells of her own journey to freedom, and know that the same outcome can be a reality for you!

After each story, you will find practical questions that will help you determine your own feelings about issues in your life, and perhaps help you get to the root cause of these issues. I encourage you to go over your answers with a trusted friend or mentor who can help guide you along the pathway to freedom and answer any questions that you might have along the way.

As you take the next step to break free from the bondage of an eating disorder, pray that God will open your heart so that you can identify the root issues at hand. Let God restore hope to your life as you embrace true and lasting freedom.

*Chapter One*

# BONNIE'S STORY: I BELIEVED THE LIES

As a young child, I loved to laugh, play, joke around, and have fun. However, as I grew older, things changed. Through different situations that happened, I began believing lies that almost destroyed my life. As these lies took root in my heart, they began to affect the way I saw myself, how I treated other people, how I viewed Jesus, and simply, how I lived my life.

One lie that I believed from a very early age was "*I am fat and ugly, so no one can love me.*" As a young child, I wore glasses and a retainer for my teeth. Kids at school and on the bus ride home did the typical teasing and name calling, making jokes about my face and about my bottom. Comments about being chubby and eating too much dessert drove my self-esteem down into the ground. In 4th grade, I began sneaking my mom's measuring tape for sewing into the back room to measure my stomach after meals to make sure I didn't get any bigger. When my older sister, whom I looked up to a lot, set a weight goal for herself, I decided to make that my goal weight as well, ignoring the fact that I was much taller than she was.

In the media and in our culture, thinness seems to be the ultimate goal to be achieved. Jokes and mockery can commonly be heard about people who are overweight, so I automatically equated looks with being loved and accepted. Thinking I looked ugly and fat, I assumed that I was unlovable and unacceptable. This made it very difficult to make friends or even talk to people. As a result of feeling so horrible about myself, I had very few friends, was lonely, shy, and withdrawn.

As I pushed people away in my anger and confusing mess of emotions inside, I also pushed Jesus out of my life and heart. As a result, it seemed that Jesus was very far away, distant, and cold. Again, Satan planted a lie, "God is angry at you," and I believed it even though I was not sure what I had done. I lived under an extremely heavy weight of guilt and condemnation that followed me everywhere I went. Many nights in elementary school, I stayed up late into the night begging God to forgive me. I grew angry at God. In my heart, I thought that God loved everyone but me.

I tried to appease God's anger and ease the guilt by working for His love. Again, I believed a lie that "once I'm good enough and have accomplished enough, then Jesus will accept me." If I volunteered more at church, talked to people more, looked prettier, got the highest grades at school, and scored the most points in sports, then maybe I would be acceptable to Jesus. I set unattainable goals for myself and spent many late nights finishing school projects that had to be perfect. The next morning, exhausted, I would try to get up early to read the Bible and pray before school. I volunteered at summer day camp with my church. I did chores around the house, helped out on the farm, and did things for my family. I had a very hard time saying no to anybody's request for fear of letting them down, and worse, letting God down.

Although I had restricted some food in junior high, it was at the end of 11th grade that I consciously decided to lose weight. I would not become overweight, like some people. I would stay in control! I had everything perfectly figured out. Little did I know that a few months later, this decision would control me. Before I knew it, my life revolved around food and exercise. I formed very strict rules about what I could and could not eat, and if I disobeyed my rules, I punished myself with even more exercise and additional restriction at the next meal. The rules were never strict enough to take away the guilt, condemnation, and shame that I felt for who I was.

As my life became increasingly more about food, I continued pushing people out of my life. Growing up, I enjoyed doing things with my family, but now, angry and ashamed of myself, I just wanted to be alone. I spent a lot of time in my room or outside. My sister and I used to stay up late chatting, but not anymore. I was very sensitive to people's words, and there was hardly anything my mom could say to me that wouldn't trigger the anger inside me. I seldom talked to my brother or dad. Physically, I was living with my family, but relationally,

I was separated from them. My whole life revolved around how little I could eat and how much I could exercise. I was weighing myself constantly. My weight began to drop and my health became very unstable. I became afraid of food because I thought it would make me fat. I did not even want to take communion at church because I was afraid it would make me gain weight.

My friends, unsure of how to respond to this, were very quiet around me. In my view, they pulled away from me, when in reality I was pulling away from them. I stopped hanging out with them and definitely did not want to go to parties because there would be food there. I had nothing to say to people and I did not want anyone to say anything to me. The only people I trusted were two older friends who had also struggled with eating disorders and we are now living in victory. I knew I could be honest with them about how I was feeling. I knew they would not freak out when I told them I wanted to die, hated life, and was angry at God.

When the doctors told me I was dying, I thought, "Good! I don't want to live!" The only sadness I felt was when I saw tears in my dad's eyes when he heard the doctor's words. At that point, my body was very weak and frail, but it was only when my body started shutting down that I finally agreed to receive professional help. Professional help consisted of different counselors who blamed everyone else in my life for my problems. As my health declined, I was finally admitted as a patient in a psychiatric ward. It was a dark, miserable, hopeless place. Everything was about food. Therapy consisted of analyzing my problems and blaming everybody else for the struggles I was facing. As soon as I reached the goal weight set by the doctors, I was sent home, only to continue living out my life of death. I was losing weight fast. Instead of freedom, all I had really learned were more rigid rules about food and exercise.

One day I watched an oncoming truck approach me and was desperately trying to gather up the courage to step out in front of it. I did not want to live this miserable life any longer. However, it seemed like there was a wall preventing me from doing it. Later, when I asked Jesus where He was that afternoon, He clearly showed me that He was that wall. He was standing between me and that truck, His arms open wide, holding me back on the sidewalk in safety.

My older sister was also struggling with an eating disorder during this time. She applied to Mercy Ministries and was accepted. If my sister was going to fly from our home in Canada to Tennessee to get real help, I certainly did not want to be left out. So, I applied as well.

I thought Mercy would make me gain weight and then send me home, just like other programs, but I found out they cared about me a whole lot more than that. It was at Mercy that I encountered Jesus, the God who created me and loves me intensely. I learned to run to Jesus instead of away from Him when I was hurt or angry. I did not need rules about food and exercise; I needed to meet Jesus, who is passionately in love with me.

Throughout my whole life up to that point, I had believed the enemy's lie that I was fat, ugly, and unlovable. But I found out that Jesus says, "like a lily among thorns is my darling among the maidens . . . show me your face, let me hear your voice; for your voice is sweet, and your face is lovely" (Song of Songs 2:2,14). Jesus has created me in His image, and because *He* says I am beautiful, I am beautiful! The Holy Spirit kept on bringing that revelation to my heart, bit by bit, and it completely changed how I saw myself and how I saw other people. This even changed my view of going to the mall. I dreaded going to the mall and I hated trying on clothes, but by the end of my stay at Mercy, I enjoyed buying new pretty clothes. It was kind of fun! Knowing what Jesus thinks about me in my heart and mind gave me confidence to talk to the other girls at Mercy, and soon, I formed some very precious friendships. I found I could enjoy hanging out with the other girls, laughing, talking, playing sports, and encouraging one another.

Being able to build friendships helped further destroy the lie that "I am forgotten and unnoticed." Zephaniah 3:17 says that Jesus takes great delight in *me*. Jesus does not just notice my sister, friends, or Mercy staff. Jesus notices and delights in ME! As the Holy Spirit revealed this truth to me, I began hungering for more of Jesus. I loved my time alone with Him in the morning, talking to Him, reading His Word, and listening to His Spirit. I began discovering that Jesus is not mean, but rather full of joy, love, and safety.

As I spent more time with Jesus and opened my heart to Him in class and in counseling sessions, He also showed me that He accepts me right now, just how I am—not when I have finished every task on my "to do" list and volunteered with every program at church—He accepts me right now, just as I am. Ephesians 2:8 says, "For it is by grace you have been saved, through faith—and this not from yourselves, it is the gift of God—not by works, so that no one can boast." My righteousness comes from Jesus Christ. He died for my sins and it is His blood that covers me and makes me righteous. This released me from having to *do* everything and to perform perfectly. Jesus released me from the heavy burden of condemnation that was weighing my heart down (Rom. 8:1). Having Jesus reveal His Truth to my heart brought so much release, so much joy! I could not remember being so happy and carefree in a very long time. I loved life and I loved waking up in the morning with my first thought being, "I am the righteousness of God in Christ Jesus. Thank you, Lord!"

Believing these truths brought tremendous freedom to my life in every area, but it was extremely hard to get to that place of trusting God and His promises. The hardest part of my time at Mercy was facing the anger that I had toward God. I always covered it up. I knew how to pretend. However, I could not keep it inside me any longer.

During my stay at Mercy, my oldest sister passed away. During my struggle with anorexia, she had gone through many rounds of treatments for breast cancer, which I had emotionally detached myself from. When I came back to Mercy after the funeral, all the anger that I had towards God finally surfaced and I had no clue what to do with it. There was a war inside my heart and my mind felt so confused and fuzzy. How could I trust a God who would let my sister die? It reinforced the lie I had believed as a young child that God was angry at me. However, we were doing a Bible Study by Beth Moore called "Believing God." It really challenged me to do exactly that—believe God, even when I do not understand. Jesus kept drawing me to Himself and when I was at home for Christmas break, I finally gave up fighting Jesus and chose to trust Him. Jesus proved Himself faithful! He has never let me down.

Finding safety and rest in Jesus was extremely important to me after I graduated from Mercy. Outside of Mercy, there are many decisions to be made. Life gets busy, and I have been hurt, but in Jesus' presence there is a refuge, a safe place. At Mercy, I had also come to love praise and worship times. This is something I found I could do at home. Whether it is soaking in God's presence in a church service, singing along to a CD, or playing guitar, Jesus meets with me and refreshes my heart through times of worship.

Another principle that helped me a lot at home was exchanging lies for truth. By believing that Jesus completely accepts and loves me, He gave me courage to start new friendships. In believing Jesus' promise in Isaiah 54:4 that I will not suffer shame, He gave me the strength to reconnect with friends I had previously shoved out of my life. Spending time alone with Jesus every day and reading His Word was very important at Mercy, and by applying that to my life at home, I have found that I've grown stronger in the truth and in understanding Jesus' love for me.

Once at home, temptations came to restrict at meals and to over exercise. I felt defeated and discouraged, but "thanks be to God, who always leads us in triumphal procession in Christ . . ." (2 Cor. 2:14) and, "being confident of this, that he who began a good work in you will carry it on to completion until the day of Christ Jesus" (Phil. 1:6), I continued to do the things I had learned at Mercy.

Being honest with my accountability partner was very important to overcoming temptation. I sometimes thought I could overcome it by myself, but I couldn't. I needed Jesus to be my strength. I needed Jesus to open a way of escape for me and He often did that through my willingness to talk and pray with my accountability partner. I also found that simply attending church was not enough; I needed fellowship. I was invited to join a cell group at my church and I agreed to go, even though I did not really know anyone there. I was surprised at the warm, loving welcome I received.

Today, I am living the life I had completely given up on before I went to Mercy. I did not just find freedom from anorexia, I found a relationship with Jesus Christ, the One who loves me. He always provides what I need at the very moment I need it. I can smile now. I can laugh and have fun again! I have been able to reconnect with many of my friends, as well as build new friendships. I am learning to have a relationship with my parents and siblings again—for which I am very thankful and excited, because I thought it was ruined forever.

I had given up the hope of ever going to a university and getting my nursing degree, but now, because of Jesus in my life, I am excited to share that I am in my second year of nursing school!

**—Bonnie**

## Personal Study Guide—How does this apply to my life?

1. The words that other people say can have a devastating effect on you when you believe them. What have people said to you that has influenced how you see yourself?

_____

_____

_____

_____

_____

2. Have there been any changes in your behavior since those things were said to you? If so, what have those changes been?

_____

_____

_____

_____

_____

3. The effects of believing any lie have the power to destroy you, but a lie only has power over you if you choose to believe it. What does John 8:32 say about the power of believing truth?

_____

_____

_____

_____

_____

4. This power comes not only from believing the truth that you receive by reading the Word of God, but also from your speaking the Word of God out loud. Isaiah 43:1–7 is a passage in the Bible that illustrates how valuable you are to God.

   Write out these verses below and practice speaking the truth out loud. Let the voice of truth drown out the lies you have believed.

   _____

   _____

   _____

   _____

   _____

5. Looking back on the time that Bonnie almost stepped in front of a moving truck, she asked the Lord where He was during that moment. God's faithfulness to Bonnie to show her where He was brought so much healing to her.

   As you are faced with a painful memory from your own life, ask God to show you where His hand was in that situation. He may speak to your heart by bringing a passage of scripture to your mind, or He may give you a picture of how He was protecting you. Write down what you remember and the emotions that the memory brings up. As you allow yourself to be open and honest, God will begin to heal that wound in your heart. Find a mature Christian counselor or friend to walk through this process with you.

   _____

   _____

   _____

   _____

_____

6. How does the truth that God revealed to you in that painful memory change what you believe about yourself, God, or other people in your life?

_____

_____

_____

_____

_____

## Talk to God

Use this space to write down any prayers, thoughts, or feelings you may have. This is a place to journal how you really feel.

_____

_____

_____

_____

_____

_____

_____

_____

_____

_____

_____

_____

# Scripture to Study:

"I tell you the truth, whoever hears my word and believes him who sent me has eternal life and will not be condemned; he has crossed over from death to life."

—John 5:24

*Chapter Two*

# LESLI'S STORY: LONGING FOR LOVE

*A* life controlled by an eating disorder is no life at all. I had bought into the lie that an eating disorder would provide love, acceptance, worth, value, and beauty for me. The idea started when an ex-boyfriend cheated on me with a girl who was anorexic. As a result of that experience, I believed that being really skinny would get me the love and attention I desired.

My parents divorced when I was 14 years old and from then on, my world turned upside down and was everything but stable. I started out struggling with anorexia, but I got tired of not eating and developed bulimia as an attempt to get the best of both worlds. During this time of destruction, I felt my life had no purpose at all, so I started doing drugs, drinking alcohol, and looking to unhealthy relationships to numb the pain.

My boyfriend at the time became my identity, as I was dating him to give me worth and value. Relying on the instability of that relationship was like relying on shifting sand. I was very insecure and had a lot of difficulty with school. After graduating from high school, it was very hard not having the routine that I was used to in high school. I didn't think I could go to college or make something of myself and I didn't have anyone there to encourage me. I needed someone to believe in me when I did not believe in myself or my ability to succeed.

My family was absent emotionally, as they were dealing with their own issues at the time. I felt overlooked, which was OK in a way because I wanted to do my own thing and roll around in the "pig pen" mess of a life that I had. The biggest problem was the lack of communication in my family. I never learned how to communicate as a result of this, and it became a hindrance for me. I lacked conflict resolutions skills because I never saw my parents work any problems out. I never got to see how to resolve conflicts. This led me to a life of avoidance and I began to avoid everything. I thought if I didn't talk about something then it didn't exist.

Confusion seemed to be my biggest companion. No matter how hard I tried to cover up my misery and pain, confusion covered my face like a veil. I hit rock bottom many different times and tried to get better on my own. Much to my dismay, I did not break free from the eating disorder, as I wanted to.

The year 2000 marked the beginning of my personal journey with the Lord. He delivered me instantly from drugs, negative relationships, and alcohol—which was wonderful—but I was still in bondage to the eating disorder, and was extremely frustrated. Like most people, I wanted God to deliver me instantly from the eating disorder, but the truth is that although freedom is always available, there is a process.

I got to a point of complete hopelessness and helplessness and had no direction for my life. I could not even keep a job because my issues were always getting in the way. In the midst of the eating disorder, my supervisor had approached me one morning after messing up some files and making a lot of mistakes and errors. He couldn't understand what the problem was, because all he was asking me to do were basic administrative tasks.

Without eating properly, I was not able to think clearly and I felt stupid for making so many mistakes. He was willing to work with me and explain things again and again, but at that point, I knew that I needed help. I saw how crazy the eating disorder was making me. I came to the pivotal point where I truly knew I didn't want to live like that anymore. I contemplated suicide, not because I wanted to die—I really wanted to live—but I knew that I could not live like that, and I didn't know how to pull myself out of it.

I reached out one more time and called my dad to tell him what was going on. Ironically, he had already called his pastor two weeks prior and was in anguish, knowing that I was struggling. His pastor had told him about Mercy Ministries. He had never said anything to me because he was waiting for my willing heart to reach out for help, knowing that no one could do it for me.

I entered the Mercy Ministries program in 2003 and stayed there nine months. Mercy equipped me with many great tools and taught me how to maintain victory and healing in Christ, but the program did not do the work for me. I actually had to press into God myself and take ownership and responsibility for my healing process. To be honest, after graduating from Mercy, I did struggle with going back to some of the old eating disorder behaviors. The victory came when I looked to God and used the tools the staff had taught me. I used the resources available to me and learned to walk on my own without needing someone to constantly hold my hand. Some people get stuck because they do not want to grow in maturity or take personal responsibility for their actions.

As I went through the program, a turning point for me was learning to renew my mind, because I realized I was walking in bondage by believing so many lies. I was able to get through meals out of sheer obedience and doing a lot of things in spite of my fear. I had to learn that I could not depend on my feelings, because if I was looking for the feeling to inspire me to be obedient, it was most likely not going to happen. I also wrote key scriptures on note cards and took them to the table with me. In the beginning, I had to read the scripture as I took each bite. I got through my meals bite by bite for the first couple of weeks until I could recall the scriptures by memory and be sustained by the strength they supplied.

From my experiences of falling and getting back up again, I have learned some very valuable lessons that have set me free from an eating disorder: I spend time in prayer every morning and ask God to search my heart. I verbally declare my submission to God every morning because His Word says that as we submit to Him and resist the devil, that the devil has to flee (see James 4:7). I ask God to help me eat in a balanced way every day, and if I am struggling with the temptation to give in to the eating disorder, I immediately call my accountability partners and verbalize the lie or temptation I am facing. I do not keep foods in my house that I know I struggle with. If I want a treat, I simply go and get one.

This is a key principle: Know your weakness and guard against it. If I do struggle with over eating on any given day, I ask God for His help.

I focus on God's strength and not my weakness, praying that God will help me be satisfied with exactly what I need. I do not isolate myself from others. I have healthy, godly friends in my life and I stay connected to church and small groups. Forming structure was very important. I got involved in my church and in core groups—I had to be plugged in. Knowing that I had to give an account for my actions made me think twice before I gave in to my struggle. I found people that I was able to process my feelings with and be held accountable to.

One thing I learned is that healing is a process. I fell after I graduated from Mercy and it created a lot of torment and anguish. I heard people say that even if you fall, just get back up. But when I actually experienced it, it was hard and discouraging. However, I learned that the times that you fall can be used as opportunities to learn and grow.

During my time at Mercy, there were certain muscles that I built, much like someone does when they are running. However, when you ride a bike you develop different muscles than when you are running. The same is true about the process you have to go through after you graduate from Mercy. It's a completely different kind of muscular development. You may be able to do Mercy, but can you do life? Mercy itself was not the answer, but they introduced me to Jesus and gave me the tools to walk life out in freedom.

God took my eight year battle with an eating disorder and turned it into an opportunity for me to develop a greater dependence upon Him. My greatest trials have produced the most intimate times I have had with the Lord. They are so precious to me, because when I had nothing, I had Him, and He is enough! Those years were not wasted and I would not trade them for anything. God has given me a full life. I graduated from college, and now I am on staff at Mercy Ministries. Every day I counsel girls who are sitting exactly where I was. In the midst of my storm, I used to tell God that if I ever overcame the eating disorder I would help other girls overcome it as well. Now, I am thrilled to say I am holding up my end of the bargain—all because of God's faithfulness.

**—Lesli**

# Personal Study Guide—How does this apply to my life?

1. Lesli believed that becoming very thin would bring her the love and attention she desired. When have you tried to change your outward appearance in order to feel loved and accepted by others?

   _____

   _____

   _____

   _____

   _____

2. What was the result of this attempt to earn the love and acceptance of others and how did it make you feel?

   _____

   _____

   _____

   _____

3. The only love that will never fail you is the love of God. When have you felt abandoned by God?

   God wants you to express your true emotions He can bring truth to them. Even though you may have felt abandoned by God, the truth is that He has never left you, so as you choose to believe the truth, your emotions will begin to line up with what you believe. What truth do you read about God's love in 1 Corinthians 13:8?

   _____

   _____

   _____

_____

_____

4. God often brings people into our lives to demonstrate His love for us, but it's important to see them as a vessel of God's love. The problem with depending on other people for love and acceptance is that only God will ever be perfectly consistent in your life. What does Psalms 100:5 say about the love and faithfulness of God?

_____

_____

_____

_____

_____

5. Lesli realized that she had to take responsibility for her own healing process. What steps do you need to take to make choices to be healthy for yourself? An example may be to set up accountability before, during, or after you eat, or you may need to simply start being honest with someone you trust about your struggle.

_____

_____

_____

_____

_____

6. Lesli also recognized her own areas of weakness and listed several ways that she could be proactive in her battle for freedom. Make a list of the areas where you are more likely to struggle, then on the opposite side, counter that weakness with a practical way to prevent falling back into the cycle of an eating disorder.

1. _____     1. _____
   _____        _____
   _____        _____

2. _____     2. _____
   _____        _____
   _____        _____

3. _____     3. _____
   _____        _____
   _____        _____

# Talk to God

Use this space to write down any prayers, thoughts, or feelings you may have. This is a place to journal how you really feel.

_____

_____

_____

_____

_____

_____

_____

_____

_____

_____

_____

_____

_____

# Scripture to Study:

"My grace is all you need. My power works best in weakness. So now I am glad to boast about my weaknesses, so that the power of Christ can work through me."

—2 Corinthians 12:9

*Chapter Three*

# HEATHER'S STORY: IT'S NOT A PERFECT WORLD

On the surface, I had it all together. I grew up in a Christian home, and thought I knew everything about God. I could tell you all the right answers and seemed to know all the "right" things to say. I asked Jesus into my heart when I was five years old because I was afraid that I would go to Hell. I knew in my heart that Jesus was my Savior and I was going to Heaven, but that was about it. I didn't have any concept of the abundant life God had for me here on earth, and my identity was wrapped up in the fact that I was a good Christian kid. I didn't swear, drink, or smoke, and I went to church every Sunday, but I did not have any concept of what it meant to have a true relationship with God. I was a regular "Bible-thumping goodie-two-shoes," and I was proud of it. Very proud.

My family did the best they could with what they had, but just like every other family, we had our share of dysfunction. Our family history of addictions and bondages included alcoholism, eating disorders, and mental illness, along with physical, emotional, and sexual abuse. It was enough for even my young naïve mind to know that something was not right.

As a family, we were in a lot of pain, and I knew it, but no one talked about it. As a matter of fact, everyone acted as though our world was perfect, especially around other Christians. Coincidentally, perfection was what I strove for. In everything I did, I tried so hard to be the perfect little Christian girl I was "supposed" to be. When my parents asked how everything was at school, I would say it was great, even though deep down, I was really hurt by the way kids picked on me for my big hair and chubby cheeks.

I was embarrassed, ashamed, and so confused. I had so much shame and hatred toward myself, but I wouldn't dare share it with anyone. Instead, I worked hard at my school work, earned the lead roles in the school musicals, sang on the worship team at church, taught Sunday school, and talked about Jesus and how much He loved everyone around me. In reality, when I would sing "Jesus loves me" and quote scripture, I had no *real* concept of the love of Jesus in my own life.

My acting skills managed to carry me through my false "perfect world" all the way to my junior year of high school, when I began dating for the first time. My boyfriend became my source of security and affirmation. I was so desperate for someone to *really* know me that I was willing to do just about anything in order to be close to him. I began lying to my parents about where I was going, skipping school, and willingly putting myself in situations of compromise.

Soon, word got out about the intimate side of our relationship and my "good little girl" identity was shattered by the vicious rumors that circulated throughout our high school and youth group. My shame and self-hatred grew, and the only way I knew how to handle it was to continue looking to my boyfriend for my sole sense of identity. Six months later, the relationship ended in an emotionally violent way and my world crashed around me. Without my "perfect girl" mask protecting me any longer, I was vulnerable and completely *alone*. I became extremely depressed and stopped eating for almost two weeks.

During my depression-induced fast, I lost quite a bit of weight and my friends and family complimented me on my slimmer and more "fit" appearance. When I began eating again, however, I found myself turning to food to numb the pain of loneliness, isolation, self-hatred, and shame, and I quickly regained the weight I'd lost. The compliments I'd been receiving quickly ceased, and instead I was confronted by concerned friends and family, commenting that I was beginning to fill out my clothes a bit and that maybe I should start to cut back on what I was eating and try to exercise a bit more—so I did.

I basically poured all of my energy into my new diet and was very successful. By the end of my first semester of college, I'd dropped a tremendous amount of weight without even realizing it. Returning home for Christmas, my family was surprised at my appearance, but I still appeared healthy. They applauded my efforts, but advised me not to lose any more weight when I returned to school. It was too late. My habits seemed irreversible, and I was in severe bondage to a full-blown eating disorder.

About a month into my second semester, I was still losing weight, and was visibly doing pretty poorly. My roommates and the campus leadership became very concerned about my health, and I was dismissed from school to go home and get help. Shortly thereafter, I was admitted to a psychiatric hospital, where I spent the majority of the next year. The hospital was a very frightening place at first. I didn't see that I had any need to be there and all I saw was a "diet-gone-wrong" . . . nothing was wrong with me. I wanted to get out of there as quickly as I could, so I did everything they told me to, telling myself that I could lose any weight I gained when they let me out. My body, however, was so severely malnourished that it was very resistant to gaining weight.

Consequently, I ended up being in the hospital longer than was ideal, and I acclimated myself to my surroundings. The staff in the hospital tried everything they could to help me and the other patients there, but when I look back on it, there was really no hope they could offer except to help us learn about nutrition and how to eat right, to get us to a healthy weight, and to send us back out to try it on our own.

The counselors were able to help me identify "root issues" of abuse, self-hatred, destructive learned behaviors, and legalistic thinking, but all they did about them was *identify* them, tell me to get angry about them, and that was it. I became a very bitter, angry, hateful person toward everyone I cared about, and I beat my family up verbally and emotionally through family counseling sessions and therapy. At one point, I was on seven different psychotropic drugs that numbed the pain and confusion so much that I don't even have a clear memory of that portion of my life.

During that time I became complacent, and although I was compliant and did everything I was asked to do to work toward "recovery," internally I really didn't see any hope for my situation. I was a prisoner of my own mind and I hated myself, the world, and everyone around me. I didn't even know if I believed in God anymore, although I kept my Bible on my nightstand and wrote letters to Him every morning, just in case He was still out there somewhere. That slight seed of hope was all I had to cling to, and I clung with all my might.

Around Christmas time during my second hospitalization, my room-mate in the hospital was discharged with an excellent prognosis. It was the type of situation where the doctors felt that if anyone would make it, she would. She was a healthy weight and appeared to be very happy externally. Everyone thought she was going to be great. Two weeks after her return home, however, we received word that she had died of a deliberate drug overdose. Apparently, she didn't have it together as much as everyone had thought, and I came to the grim realization that this really wasn't a game—this was life or death.

That day, the staff and counselors at the hospital sat us all down and laid out some pretty grim hopeless facts. They gave us the statistics, stating that one in four of us would most likely die from our eating disorders, that one in ten of us might have a shot at living a normal life again, but that the remaining ninety percent would probably be in and out of institutions for the rest of our lives, so we should pretty much buckle in for the ride. This moment was my breaking point.

As I finally came face to face with my brokenness, my mind was suddenly flooded with the scriptures I'd learned growing up. Jeremiah 29:11 specifically began circulating through my mind: "'I know the plans I have for you,' declares the Lord, 'They're plans to prosper you and not to harm you, plans to give you hope and a future.'" At the same moment, I saw a vision of a balancing scale; that promise from God was on one side, and the doctors' statistics on the other. Suddenly, I realized I had a decision to make: I could believe what the world was telling me, that I was a hopeless case, or I could take God at His word and believe that He had a hope, future, and plan for my life. In that defining moment, I decided to give God one more chance, and I started praying for a way of escape. I started praying that God would help me find life again. That's when God brought me to Mercy Ministries.

I had never heard of Mercy Ministries before, but within two weeks of initially crying out to God, the ministry's name crossed my radar screen three different times. I began to wonder if this was my answer, so I filled out an application figuring I had nothing to lose. I soon discovered I had everything to gain. Three months later, I walked through the doors of Mercy and I will never ever be the same.

It would take years to fully describe what God did in my life during the months I spent at Mercy. God turned my world upside-down and right-side up. When I walked through the doors of Mercy, my head was hanging down in shame, and I've been told my face was clouded with sadness. Although I believed my spirit had made a decision to choose life and run to healing, it took a long time for my flesh to comply and obey.

From day one, I was attacked with doubt and unbelief, but these feelings were only the first of many hurdles on my run to freedom. I would look at the other girls around me that had different issues and see in scripture how God could heal them, but I saw *nothing* in scripture about eating disorders. How was I supposed to believe that God could help me? One day, after listening to Nichole Nordeman's song, "Help Me Believe," I was reading in the Psalms and the Holy Spirit illuminated Psalm 107:18–21: "They loathed all food, and drew near the gates of death. Then they cried to the Lord in their trouble, and he saved them from their distress. He sent forth His Word and healed them; He rescued them from the grave. Let them give thanks to the Lord for His unfailing love and His wonderful deeds for men." At that moment, my eyes were opened, and I realized through this scripture that God had promised to set *me* free. It was His *Word* that would heal me, so I dedicated myself to filling my mind with the truth of His Word. God began to help me recognize the lies that were feeding into the shame and self-hatred that penetrated my being. As I discovered these lies about myself, God, and others, I learned to replace them with the truth that was so clearly written in the Bible.

All in all, while I was at Mercy, I learned how to love. I learned to love God, others, and myself with pure motives and a heart that seeks after God, not for selfish desires or self-protection. God fulfills my heart's desires and He is all the protection I'll ever need. I get so excited when I think about these lessons, along with the thousands of others that God taught me during my time at Mercy. Yes, I did learn to eat and take care of myself in a healthy way again, but even greater was the internal healing God did in my heart.

Since my graduation from Mercy, God has continued to do amazing things in my life. As I've continued to trust in Him, He's provided me with an amazing family of friends who are seeking after Him in the same way I am. They are people who love me for who I am in spite of my shortcomings, and support me in the areas of my weakness. For the first time in my life, I have real friends.

God has also taught me to trust Him for everything in my life, not only the things I need like finances, a job, and health (although He's been so faithful to provide those things), but also the things I desire. God has fulfilled my dreams, and it's been amazing to watch His hand on my life. There's no earthly way I could have orchestrated or manipulated the circumstances in my life so they'd turn out the way they have, but by placing everything in God's hands, I have literally watched my dreams become a reality.

Life is by no means easy. I still have struggles, and I know I'll never be perfect. I would be lying if I didn't admit that there are still days when I look in the mirror and hate what I see. I have even had my moments of wondering if it's even worth it to go on. The difference is, that when I find myself in that place, *I don't stay there and I don't give in to the lies.* In the past, thoughts like these would echo and cycle into a black hole of hopelessness, but now I cling to the words of 2 Corinthians 10:3–5, "For though we walk in the flesh, we are not waging war according to the flesh. For the weapons of our warfare are not of the flesh but have divine power to destroy strongholds. We destroy arguments and every lofty opinion raised against the knowledge of God, and take every thought captive to obey Christ." Before a thought even has the chance to take root in my mind, I know I must actively choose to reject it as a lie and replace it with the truth. I prepare myself for battle by keeping my mind filled with the TRUTH of God's Word. Then these counterfeit thoughts are clearly identified as lies.

In difficult times, I also cling to the truth that there is *beauty* in the struggle. After all, it's the struggle that keeps me clinging to God, and when I spend time in His presence, I find myself strangely grateful that life *isn't* easy; because it makes my relationship with God *that* much stronger! I resonate with Paul's sentiments in 2 Corinthians 1:9–10: "Indeed, we felt that we had received the sentence of death. But that was to make us rely not on ourselves but on God who raises the dead. He delivered us from such a deadly peril, and He will deliver us. On Him we have set our hope that *He will deliver us again.*" Reading truth like this gives me so much hope in knowing that as long as I seek after God, *He* will never let me go!

After all, life is *not* a destination lived in perfection; it is a journey of seeking after God. It's a wild adventure to know Him and be known by Him. I'm learning to fall in love with Him and cling to Him more and more every day. With each trial, I am more aware of my need for the Lord, so I seek Him further. In retrospect, I can clearly see that God took what the enemy meant for harm and is using it for His good! Today, I believe that I am seeing myself more and more through God's eyes—as a beautiful young woman with a hope and future, and as a woman set apart for God's work. I am a worshipper and friend of God. God has given me my life back, and I can do nothing less than dedicate each precious day to worshiping Him.

—**Heather**

## Personal Study Guide—How does this apply to my life?

1.  Heather thought that as a Christian she was expected to both *be* perfect as well as *act* like everything was perfect in her imperfect life. When have you felt the same pressure to appear perfect, hiding what was really going on inside?

_____

_____

_____

_____

_____

2. How has pretending to be perfect and denying the problems with yourself or within your family affected you? How has it affected your relationships with others?

_____

_____

_____

_____

_____

3. The reality is that neither you nor the world around you will ever be perfect, but pretending that it is, will only delay the healing work that God wants to do in your life. What does God say about His ability to work when you allow yourself to be open and vulnerable with Him in 2 Corinthians 12:9?

_____

_____

_____

_____

_____

4. Denying that there is a problem will only prevent you from receiving help. For Heather, this almost led to her death. The need for appearing that you "have it all together" is often rooted in pride, as you are unwilling to admit that you need help. What does 1 Peter 5:5–6 say about how God views a prideful heart?

_____

_____

_____

_____

_____

5. God says that He gives grace to the humble. As you humble yourself before the Lord, you are opening a door for not only His grace, but also for His powerful healing. A great way to humble yourself is to acknowledge your need for Him in every area of your life. Write down the different areas or situations in your life in which you know you need God's grace. Pray through each of these with a trusted friend or counselor, thanking God for the grace that He is bringing to you as you release each situation to Him.

_____

_____

_____

_____

_____

6. Even though life may not be perfect, as Heather came to realize, there is beauty in the struggle. God will use each time that the enemy tries to come against you as an opportunity to turn it around for your good. What things would you like to see restored in your life?

_____

_____

_____

_____

_____

## Talk to God

Use this space to write down any prayers, thoughts, or feelings you may have. This is a place to journal how you really feel.

_____

_____

_____

_____

_____

_____

_____

_____

_____

_____

_____

_____

_____

## Scripture to Study:

"Therefore, as God's chosen people, holy and dearly loved, clothe yourselves with compassion, kindness, humility, gentleness and patience."

—Colossians 3:12

*Chapter Four*

# CRYSTAL'S STORY: A BATTLE FOR CONTROL

Growing up in an unstable and abusive childhood, I felt that I did not have much value or self-worth. I did not know how to handle the pain and rejection that life brought through other people's choices and those of my own.

My mother left when I was three and moved off with her boyfriend, leaving me to live with my great-grandmother. My brother and I visited our mother only on holidays and during the summer. After my mother remarried when I was six, the environment in their home became very unstable and violent. My mother had been diagnosed as severely bipolar, and my stepfather was an alcoholic and was physically abusive to my mother and brother, and sexually abusive to me.

At the age of 12, I was framed for a crime that my mother committed during a manic episode and I was put in a juvenile detention center. After that ordeal, I was not allowed to see my mother ever again. In addition to that loss, my grandmother passed away a year later. She was my main source of love and stability throughout my entire life, and now she was gone. Everywhere I turned, I felt the lack of stability. I decided at that moment that I didn't need anyone and that I could take care of myself. I became very independent and headstrong and decided I was not going to let anyone ever run over, control, or hurt me again.

Around this same time, I began to struggle immensely with body image issues, insecurities, and low self-esteem. I became a perfectionist and based my worth on the things that I did. I worked very hard in school, excelled in my grades, and was also heavily involved in sports and other school organizations. My desire was to be the best at everything and I wanted people to notice and love me. I was always searching for acceptance.

I bounced around in high school, living with different extended family members and friends, never staying in one place for very long. I felt I was always searching for stability, love, affirmation, and a mother figure in my life. My best friend and her mom played a huge role in my life. They began picking me up each week for church, and I accepted the Lord after about a year of going to church with them.

However, my insecurities continued to develop during my sophomore year of high school. I began restricting my food intake and lost a significant amount of weight in a short period of time. People noticed and would comment on the weight loss, but no one knew the severity of the problem that was rapidly developing.

Due to my extreme involvement in sports, I could not keep up the strict starvation regimen that I had developed, so toward the end of high school, the anorexia developed into bulimia, and I was binging and purging up to three times a day. I also began severely abusing laxatives, diuretics, and an emetic drug that induced vomiting. I developed major stomach complications, and after testing, was put on medications. I had a lot of nerve damage to my intestines from the self-inflicted abuse my body had taken.

A couple of years later, I was hospitalized for an esophageal rupture. The doctors told me if I didn't get help that I could die. I refused recommendations for treatment and thought that this incident scared me enough to be my wake-up call, and I could get better on my own. Even though I did well for a few months, I quickly returned to my old habits and things progressed even further than before. I became depressed and isolated. I found ways to order prescription drugs that I could abuse to escape reality and attempt to numb the pain in addition to falling deeper into bulimia.

My life was consumed by the eating disorder and I rarely felt like being around anyone. I was always moody, depressed, and full of anxiety and fear. I really hated what I was doing, but I did not know how to change. I felt I could not stop, and I knew I was out of control.

It was hard to even function in the tasks of daily living. At that time, dying sounded like the best solution and the only way out. I knew at that point I was at the end of myself. I had exhausted all of my efforts and needed something more. I knew I needed help and that I could not do it on my own. I saw myself as a failure and was sure God saw me the same way. I was full of shame and regretted the things I had done and the things that had been done to me in the past. I hated who I was and who I had become. When I heard about Mercy Ministries, I applied as a last resort. I heard stories of girls who had been set free, and was clinging to the hope that maybe one day I could be one of them.

When I entered Mercy, I was determined to do whatever it took to get better and never look back. One of the hardest parts of my journey to freedom was letting go of control. I had devoted my whole life to maintaining control, so releasing control and learning to trust God and others was difficult. I slowly learned how to surrender every aspect of my life to God, and as a result, I began to experience His peace and an incredible sense of rest. I learned that even when things seem out of control on the outside, I can rest knowing that God is always in control of the situation.

Renewing my mind was also difficult and took a lot of work, but God is faithful and brought more and more freedom into my life as I learned to live by His promises and truths. Learning to take my thoughts captive was key. My natural tendency was to act on every thought that came up in my mind, but I learned that not all thoughts are of God. In fact, most thoughts are not Godly until we have our minds renewed to His Word. I had to be very intentional about recognizing lies from the enemy and replacing them with truth.

I learned the importance of structure and balance in my life while at Mercy. After I was back at home, I had to structure and plan my days so that I could maintain balance. Having time daily with God through praying, reading, and speaking His Word is a vital part to each day. As I do this, God fills me with fresh joy, peace, truth, and life. I also got plugged into an amazing church that is full of life. Being an active member in a healthy church is also a key component to staying strong, and having that pastoral leadership is very important. There is a strong accountability and protection that comes with being united and active in a church family.

This accountability was so important to me, because I used to struggle with so much pride and I rejected help from anyone. Having a few close Godly friends and spiritual mentors is important as you walk through both the good and the hard times in life. I learned how to lean on God and look to Him as I work through problems and issues that surface. In addition, I also learned how to discern when I need help, accountability, prayer, and wisdom from others.

Walking in freedom is wonderful and attainable, but life is real and temptations do come. I learned to find the root issue that is triggering a particular temptation, and how to create a strategy to tackle it. I learned not to turn off and tune out from what I am feeling and thinking—that is the devil's playground! In the past, I wanted to avoid pain and escape reality. I sought temporary satisfaction by ignoring my feelings, but that only led me to destructive behavior patterns.

Feelings and emotions are wonderful things that God has placed within us, but we should not be controlled by them or afraid of them. Most often, in every temptation, I could find a trigger or root behind the struggle. A few times the struggles were straight attacks of the enemy, but most often I could pinpoint some triggering factors that led to the temptation and struggle to resort to old coping behaviors. I learned to seek Godly wisdom and prayer from people I trusted. I would also find key scriptures related to the root issue and speak God's Word out loud over myself and the issue. Keeping your mind renewed and continually being in tune to your thoughts is also very important to walking in freedom. If you are struggling and cannot find a root cause, examine your thoughts—do they line up with the Word of God? If you find some that do not, study and find out what God's Word says regarding that belief, and replace it with the truth.

Freedom is real. Don't let anyone tell you that you will struggle for the rest of your life—that is a lie from the enemy. I am living proof, as are many others, that an abundant life of freedom is possible. Your past does not determine your future. My past is now a stepping stone to my future, not a stumbling block. God can make beauty from our ashes. I am living such a balanced and fruitful life. God has restored much of the lost time and resources that I wasted and is also restoring the broken relationships in my life.

God has not only healed my heart, He has also healed my body of the physical damage that occurred from the eating disorder and prescription drug use. My stomach and intestines are fully functioning with no medication (which is a miracle, because I took medication for 5 years and almost had surgery on my intestines). I no longer have a heart murmur, and my esophagus is totally healed. As I walk in obedience to God, He continually pours out blessings and provides provision for my life. God is presently leading me and giving me great passion and vision for the future.

This past year has been amazing and one of great victory and strides. I graduated from Louisiana Tech University with a degree in nutrition and dietetics. I am currently working on my Master's Degree in Nutrition Science, doing research as a graduate assistant, and working at a local hospital as a clinical dietitian/nutritionist. God is truly taking what the enemy meant to destroy me and using it for good and for His glory. I get to counsel, educate, and help others find keys to living balanced and healthy lives in the area of nutrition.

God is restoring so much in my life and bringing so many promises to pass. Right now, God is stretching me and growing me in my expertise at work. In the future, I want to minister to girls with eating disorders and various life controlling issues. I want to use my experience as a nutrition professional and my own journey of healing to help women find the path to life, freedom, and total healing in Christ.

—**Crystal**

## Personal Study Guide—How does this apply to my life?

1. When Crystal felt out of control in her unstable environment, she began focusing all of her attention on excelling in school, sports, and her destructive eating patterns. How do you react when life around you seems to be unstable and out of your control? Be specific.

_____

_____

_____

_____

_____

2. Who or what do you find yourself frustrated with when you feel out of control?

   _____

   _____

   _____

   _____

   _____

3. The reality is that the only person you have any control over is yourself. You cannot always control the *situations* in life or other people, but you are always in control of your own *reaction* to those people and situations. What does 1 Peter 3:8–12 say that you can control in response to life around you?

   _____

   _____

   _____

   _____

   _____

4. The more you try to gain control over things that you cannot, the more you will feel out of control and frustrated with life. What does God suggest that you do with the burdens in your life, according to 1 Peter 5:7?

   _____

   _____

   _____

   _____

   _____

5. When you are so focused on the problem, it is often hard to see the solution. What does God promise you in Psalm 40:2 as you release control in the midst of the chaos around you?

_____

_____

_____

_____

_____

6. Write out practical ways that you can keep your focus on God and surrender control to Him throughout your day. Be aware of times during your day when you are clinging to a false sense of control, such as with food, and practice releasing control during each meal. Do not be afraid to ask for support and accountability during those hard times!

_____

_____

_____

_____

_____

## Talk to God

Use this space to write down any prayers, thoughts, or feelings you may have. This is a place to journal how you really feel.

_____

_____

_____

_____

_____

_____

_____

_____

_____

_____

_____

_____

_____

_____

## Scripture to Study:

"Every good and perfect gift is from above, coming down from the Father of the heavenly lights, who does not change like shifting shadows."

—James 1:17

*Chapter Five*

# BETHANY'S STORY: FACING THE FEAR

lthough I was born into an incredible Christian family, circumstances brought seeds of mistrust, fear and rejection into
my life at a very young age. Because I believed there was something
inherently wrong with me, this led me to hide who I truly was and
become confused about who God had created me to be. I stuffed all
emotions of anger and hurt and hid them behind a smile and facade
of being "fine." But as Proverbs 14:13 says, "Laughter cannot mask a
heavy heart. When the laughter ends, the grief remains." When I was
12 years old, I could no longer deal with the pain and hurt I felt inside,
and I turned to anorexia to numb my aching soul.

I was present in body, but absent in every other capacity. I forfeited
building relationships with my parents and friends. After reaching a
point where my heart was beginning to fail and I was being threat-
ened with hospitalization, I begged and pleaded for my parents to
give me one more chance. This began a cycle of doctor, nutritionist,
counseling, and psychiatrist appointments which would continue for
years. As I gained weight back, I began to resort to purging behaviors
to rid myself of the disgust and shame. I was also introduced to
self-harm as a way to escape. Even though I had both academic and
athletic success, I believed I was a failure, a disappointment, and that
I would never be good enough. When I graduated high school and
went to college, I thought that everything would change. Little did
I realize, that when the problem is in you, it goes with you! I found
that no matter where I was, I created the exact same environment
for myself. By my sophomore year, I found myself in over my head
with anorexia and bulimia. This resulted in two in-patient treatment
stays. I refused to take time off from school to get healthy because

my identity was so wrapped up in what I did, and I believed that I wasn't that bad.

The summer before I started my senior year of college, I knew things had to change. I prayed that God would bring me to a place of brokenness, because I knew that I could not get there on my own. In just a short amount of time, a number of things began to happen that actually brought me to a place where I was able to humble myself and ask for help. I knew if I didn't ask for help, I wasn't going to make it.

All my life I had pushed to achieve and perform, but the fact was that I was dying. I remember praying I could just go to sleep and never wake up. My doctors told me that if I did not do something, I would die. I had had an application for Mercy Ministries filled out for several months, but I knew I could not go until I was ready. I felt like I had finally reached that point, and I went through the application process. A few months later, I walked through the doors of Mercy.

When I entered the program, I would describe myself as one who projected a well-fortified city whose walls would not come down. I feared that if people knew the real me, they would walk away. After all, I thought that I was used, dirty, and worthless. I didn't trust anyone, even God, but God began speaking to me through the teaching that I heard while I was there. One teaching in particular talked about the importance of having a progressive faith, which means that first we hear, then we trust, and then we believe. I had wondered why all of my life I could believe God's Word was true for everyone else, but not for me. The fact of the matter was I didn't trust Him or His Word. I always assumed that surely there was an ulterior motive.

Much of my time at Mercy was spent learning about the true character of God. Hebrews 6:17–19 says, "So God has given both His promise and His oath. These two things are unchangeable because it is impossible for God to lie. Therefore, we who have fled to Him for refuge can take new courage, for we can hold on to His promise with confidence. This confidence is like a strong and trustworthy anchor for our souls. It leads us through the curtain of Heaven into God's inner sanctuary." This scripture was crucial to showing me that God is faithful, good, just, slow to anger, full of grace, and abounding in love. These are not attributes of God that He can withhold as He pleases; no, they are the essence of who He is. As He began to give me a revelation of His trustworthiness, I was able to allow Him to begin to chisel away at the walls that I had used to protect myself, and other people inside my world.

One of the most liberating things that happened during my stay at Mercy was when I realized my identification was no longer as a sick girl with an eating disorder. I realized that 2 Corinthians 5:17 says, "If anyone is in Christ, he is a new creation; old things have passed away and all things have become new." I no longer saw myself as an anorexic, a bulimic, or a cutter, but rather as a beautiful daughter of the Most High God. I saw myself as an overcomer and more than a conqueror through Christ Jesus. For so long, my identity was in what I was doing, and I had no idea who I really was. Now when I fail, I know that it doesn't make me a failure. If I disappoint someone, I know I am not a disappointment.

I knew the Lord had begun an amazing work in me, but even after I left Mercy, I knew that I still had areas of my life that God was showing me how to trust Him with. Within a month of graduating, I began my first year as a veterinary student. It was during this time that God led me to Isaiah 26:3, "You will keep in perfect peace all who trust in you, whose thoughts are fixed on you!" Then He took me to the story in Mark 4:35–41 where Jesus and the disciples were in a boat during a great storm. The disciples were panicking, and Jesus was asleep in the stern of the boat. I saw in this scripture two people in the same circumstance with two completely different reactions. I looked at the difference between the two: the disciples were focused on their problem, Jesus was focused on His Father; one was in complete terror, and one was captivated by peace. Instead of walking in fear that I would be overcome by the storms and challenges of this life, I began to thank God in advance for His provision.

Life has not been perfect since leaving Mercy. During times of immense attack or when I do fall, I often refer back to Micah 7:8, "Do not rejoice over me, my enemy; When I fall, I will arise; When I sit in darkness, the Lord will be a light unto me." I often compare myself to the Israelites whenever the Lord delivered them from their slavery in Egypt. In Exodus, it says that they looked back with longing to the land that the Lord had set them free from. I have asked the Lord to show me what in my heart looks back with longing at the pit that He has lifted me out of.

In this, God is taking me to deeper levels of healing. He is working on some very tender parts of my heart that have been long shut off to anyone, including myself. During this time, His Word has become like a soothing balm to my soul. Scriptures like Isaiah 45:2, "I will go before you and make the crooked places straight; I will break in pieces the gates of bronze and cut the bars of iron. I will give you the treasures of darkness and hidden riches of secret places, that you may know that I, the Lord, who call you by name, am the God of Israel." And various Psalms like 121:1–3, "I will lift my eyes to the hills—from whence comes my help? My help comes from the Lord, who made heaven and earth. He will not allow my foot to be moved; He who keeps me will not slumber."

God has shown me how to use His Word to battle the temptations that come against me. I know that for me, there are certain areas in which I am more susceptible for attack. One is in the area of food. I plan out times for me to eat and when possible, I eat with someone else. I do not go to the bathroom right after a meal. With exercise, I have a limit that I have set for myself, and have people in my life who hold me accountable to those limits. I have to be very careful to check my motive behind working out. I ask myself, "Am I doing it because it is healthy and I want to, or am I doing it because I feel like I have to or as a form of escaping?"

Lying, silence, and deception have been major strongholds in my life, and the only way their power is broken over me is through rigorous honesty. I am only as accountable as I choose to be. Psalm 32:3–5 says, "When I refused to confess my sin, I was weak and miserable, and I groaned all day long. Day and night your hand of discipline was heavy on me. My strength evaporated like water in the summer heat. Finally, I confessed all my sins to you and stopped trying to hide them. I said to myself, 'I will confess my rebellion to the Lord.' And you forgave me! All my guilt is gone." Much like David, when I stubbornly refuse to be honest about my struggles, my joy and peace disappear. It is only when I fall before His throne and open up to those He has placed in my life, that I feel like I am walking in the abundant life Jesus died to give me.

My prayer in sharing my story is that it might be a ray of hope for those who are hopeless. Revelation 12:11 tells us, "We overcome by the blood of the Lamb and the word of our testimony." Freedom is a reality, not merely a dream. Life can be different, but you have to choose to allow God to change you. I had been told by medical professionals and counselors that I would struggle with self-destructive behaviors for the rest of my life and that I would cycle in and out of treatment. Little did they realize that God could take my brokenness and make something beautiful.

I am currently in vet school pursuing my Doctorate of Veterinary Medicine. Post-graduation from vet school, I feel called to work as a veterinarian in third world countries, and ultimately, I would love to work with other young girls who have gone through similar things. However, each day my sole purpose remains the same and can be summed up in Philippians 3:10, "For my determined purpose is that I may know Him."

—**Bethany**

## Personal Study Guide—How does this apply to my life?

1.  Bethany lived in fear that people would be able to see behind her "façade of being fine." What are some things that you fear?

_____

_____

_____

_____

_____

2.  Over time, a natural response to fear is to adapt your lifestyle to avoid being faced with the things that bring feelings of fear. Do you recognize any behaviors, habits, or routines that you do throughout the day that are rooted in fear?

_____

_____

_____

_____

_____

3.  Living controlled by fear is not God's will for your life. What does
    2 Timothy 1:7 say about what God wants us to learn to walk in
    instead of fear?

    _____

    _____

    _____

    _____

    _____

4.  God says that "perfect love casts out all fear" (1 John 4:18). The
    true meaning of love is defined in 1 Corinthians 13:4–8. As you
    read this verse, write down the definitions of love that are the most
    difficult for you to accept.

    _____

    _____

    _____

    _____

    _____

5.  With a trusted friend or counselor, ask God what painful past expe-
    riences contributed to your distorted perception of those attributes
    of love. Write what God shows you about each situation and allow
    Him to heal those painful wounds from your past.

    _____

_____

_____

_____

_____

6. How can you be intentional today to make steps in facing and
   overcoming not only the fear of dealing with your past, but also the
   fears you have regarding food and body image?

_____

_____

_____

_____

_____

## Talk to God

Use this space to write down any prayers, thoughts, or feelings you may
have. This is a place to journal how you really feel.

_____

_____

_____

_____

_____

_____

_____

_____

_____

_____

_____

_____

_____

_____

# Scripture to Study:

"Even though I walk through the valley of the shadow of death, I will fear no evil, for you are with me; your rod and your staff, they comfort me."

—Psalm 23:4

*Chapter Six*

# GIOVY'S STORY: NO NEED TO COMPARE

*I*used to think people would be disgusted if they knew the real me, so I tried to look like someone else. I saw myself as ugly, fat, worthless, and therefore, unlovable. Due to all the hurts, abuse, and rejection from my early years, I saw the world as a bad place and accepted that I was never going to be happy.

I grew up in Peru, and my parents were very wealthy and influential people. As a result of the pressure they felt to have the perfect family, they had very high standards and expected me to be the best in everything I did. I became a perfectionist and found my identity in sports and personal success. I had always seen my family and other people that I looked up to concerned about their weight, so I easily adapted to the diets that I had been around and heard about my whole life.

My parents also had high expectations for my sister, and I watched her endure the pressure to fit a mold of perfection. Being a little chubbier than I was and not as involved in sports, my sister was put on constant diets and praised whenever she managed to lose weight. Jealous of the recognition she received for her weight loss, I was determined to use the same method to capture my mom's attention and approval.

At the same time, my gymnastics coach was encouraging me to lose weight as well. I remember working so hard to prepare myself for an upcoming tournament, but as the team was about to leave, my coach announced that he was going to weigh each of us before we left. After everyone had been weighed, our coach gave us all a talk. He didn't want to embarrass the girls who needed to lose a few pounds, so he just addressed everyone as a group. He made sure that we knew that in this sport, every pound counted. Even though he told me my weight was

OK, I decided to lose some more weight, hoping to win the spot of being the coach's favorite.

The eating disorder began with just a thought, but somehow it developed into a lifestyle. It not only made me sick physically, but also emotionally and mentally. I was unable to develop normal relationships because I would always believe that people were looking at me and criticizing me for how big I was and how bad I looked. I became so consumed with the food I was eating or not eating, diet pills, laxatives, purging, and hiding food, that by the end of the day, I was too tired to go out or be around anyone. I couldn't have normal healthy relationships because I compared myself with other people and became very jealous and upset if they were thinner than I was.

My dysfunctional lifestyle also began to affect my relationship with God. To me, God was just one more person who had expectations and standards I would never be able to meet. I had failed Him so many times that I thought He had given up on me, so I gave up on myself. I was so empty and lonely on the inside and didn't know how things would ever change, so I decided that I was done hoping that they would.

One night, after a massive overdose and extensive self-harm, I passed out on my bedroom floor. For some strange reason, a friend from Australia felt an urgency to contact me right then. She could not reach me, so she called the Australian Embassy and asked them to go through the embassy in Peru to contact my parents. In her words, she "moved the whole world" to get my parent's phone number. They found me in the bathroom and rushed me to the hospital to receive help. I was not expected to live that night, but God had a different plan for me.

About that same time, my pastor's wife called and told me that an international speaker was here in Lima, Peru to speak at an annual conference held every year at our church where people come from all over the world. She explained to me that this lady had facilities in the United States and other countries that could actually help girls with issues like mine. My pastor's wife asked if I would be willing to meet with this lady. I was hesitant at first, because I had plans to go out on the town with one of my friends. However, later that night my friend cancelled our plans, so with nothing else to do, I decided I would meet this mysterious lady.

My pastor's wife picked me up and took me to our church where her friend Nancy Alcorn, founder of Mercy Ministries was speaking. After the meeting that night, she introduced me to Nancy, who had come to impart the vision of Mercy Ministries and proclaim principles of freedom in the nation of Peru. Nancy talked to me for a while about the Mercy program and encouraged me to apply. I listened to everything that she told me, and within a few weeks I was in the application process. A few months later, I was packing my bags to come to the program.

As soon as I arrived at Mercy, God started an amazing work in me. I couldn't understand how a facility that was free of charge was willing to take me in to help me—no one else had ever done that! I realized the staff at Mercy were filled with God's love and that they genuinely wanted to see me walking in freedom without asking for anything in return.

The hardest part for me in this process of freedom was to open up and trust my counselor with all of my past shameful experiences. I thought I was the only one who ever did such terrible things, but that was a lie! My counselor loved me with God's unconditional love and she told me that nothing I could do—or not do—would cause that to change. The staff at Mercy helped me see the true heart of God.

Living in freedom requires daily choices, and I have made the decision to never go back to my former way of life. Yes, I have struggles, but the Bible says I will never be tempted beyond what I can bear. Through Him, I am more than a conqueror (see Rom. 8:37; 1 Cor. 10:13). I have learned not to be satisfied with yesterday's victories because God has new victories for me every day!

At Mercy, a very valuable lesson I was taught was that I couldn't be passive any longer, but I needed to be proactive about my healing. I understood the importance of renewing my mind daily and seeing myself the way God, my Creator, sees me. I had to make the choice to believe what He says about me, and to recognize and despise the lies that the enemy tries to place in my mind. In other words, I needed to participate in my own rescue.

I learned that my past doesn't have to determine my future and that I'm a new creature in Christ—all things are new and old things have passed away (see 2 Cor. 5:17). God knows my past and the wrong choices I've made, but He does not judge me. He was right there the whole time patiently waiting with open arms for me to come to Him.

God has healed me emotionally, spiritually, and mentally. I am off of all the psychotropic medications that four different psychiatrists told me I was going to be taking for the rest of my life. It feels so good to be free from all of those medications and know that God has given me a sound mind. No matter what doctors say, there is not any diagnosis that God can't heal. The Bible said He came to heal and give us life more abundantly, which is not the life I had while I was dealing with an eating disorder! As I am experiencing life on the other side of bondage, I can honestly say freedom is real and possible.

I love my life and I don't wake up every morning wishing I was dead anymore. I wake up each morning with great anticipation to see what God has in store for me that day. I am very passionate about my love for God—hating everything He hates and loving everything He loves. His ways are way better than my ways, so I have made the decision to follow His direction, because I know He cares about every single detail of my life.

After I returned home, I saw some pictures of myself from when I was at my lowest point. It took me a minute to realize that the girl in the pictures was me! During that time, I thought I was so overweight; no matter what the scale said, I never felt like I was thin enough. Now, looking back at those pictures, I just cry as I am able to see how sick I really was, and the extent of what God has rescued me from. I am also blown away at how far from the truth my perception really was.

God has filled my heart with a passion for Him and with compassion to go out and reach others. It's time to rise up and stop the devil from writing the story of our lives! We need to make the devil regret ever trying to mess with us!

—**Giovy**

# Personal Study Guide—How does this apply to my life?

1. Giovy thought the only way that she would be accepted was to look like someone else. Do you compare yourself to others in your life? What do you feel that looking like someone else would achieve?

_____

_____

_____

_____

_____

2. What emotions do you feel toward people who seem to have the "perfect" life or body?

_____

_____

_____

_____

_____

3. The enemy can use others to cause you to be jealous and envious of what other people have or look like. Make a list of the things that you are the most dissatisfied with about your body, then get with a trusted friend or counselor and pray through each one. Ask God to give you a new perspective as you verbally thank Him for creating those areas uniquely for you.

_____

_____

_____

_____

4. When jealousy gets out of control, it affects every area of your life. Not only will it cause you to obsess over the inadequacies that you see in your own body, but it has the power to destroy relationships as it can cause your heart to grow angry and bitter. What does James 3:14–16 say about what results from envy and jealousy?

_____

_____

_____

_____

_____

5. If you are dissatisfied with how you were created, you need to take your frustrations to the one who actually created you. Resist the natural tendency to target your anger and bitterness toward the people you desire to look or be like. How is your disappointment with the way that God created you affecting the people around you, and your relationship with them?

_____

_____

_____

_____

_____

6. Know that God did not make you with flaws or mistakes, but created you in His own image! Read Psalm 139 and write down the words that God uses to describe how He created you.

_____

_____

_____

_____

_____

## Talk to God

Use this space to write down any prayers, thoughts, or feelings you may have. This is a place to journal how you really feel.

_____

_____

_____

_____

_____

_____

_____

_____

_____

_____

_____

_____

# Scripture to Study:

"Let the peace of Christ rule in your hearts, since as members of one body you were called to peace. And be thankful."
                                        —Colossians 3:15

*Chapter Seven*

# KACY'S STORY:
# UNREALISTIC EXPECTATIONS

*A*s a ballerina, I spent fourteen years trying to meet unrealistic standards the "experts" had placed on every girl who was serious about dancing. I worked so hard to please my teachers, but could never reach "perfection." As a result, I had very low self-esteem and hated myself. My dance teachers physically and verbally abused me. I developed an eating disorder to cope with feeling worthless and invaluable. Life at home was difficult. I was also being verbally and physically abused by my brothers, and my dad stayed emotionally disconnected from me. In addition to this, my mom worked all of the time, which left me longing to be loved.

My concept of God and the church was very warped. Due to the abuse in my past, I thought God would strike me with lightning if I did anything wrong. I was terrified of Him. My church only confirmed my distorted perception of God when they kicked me out and told me they were done with me. While there are many good churches across America, unfortunately there are some that aren't so good.

I also struggled with homosexuality and self-harm at the time, but the people in my church did not even try to understand my issues. Seeing me as nothing more than an anorexic girl who was confused about her sexual identity and cut herself, they judged me and sent me away. A family I knew had a daughter in the program at Mercy Ministries, and they told me about Mercy. As a result, I started looking into the program, and within a few months I had gone through the application process and was accepted into the program.

When I arrived at Mercy, it was very important for me to renew my mind with what God says about who I am and to let His truth replace all of the twisted lies I had programmed into my mind. During my struggle with the eating disorder, I made a book and printed out quotes and pictures I found on a pro-eating disorder web site. I basically brainwashed myself to think food was "bad" and that I was worthless unless I looked emaciated. Yet, at Mercy, I learned about God's love for me, even with all of my attitudes and quirks. He knows the number of hairs on my head, my favorite flower, number, color, and smell, and cares about every detail of my life.

At Mercy, I also learned about generational patterns. I had never heard of these before, but when I found out what they were, I was shocked! It explained so much of why my parents made the mistakes that they did, and why I had fallen into the same cycles of sin that my family had. The generational patterns in my life were a major part of my bondage. I was prone to confusion with my sexual identity and mental disorders. When I prayed through these things in counseling, I found freedom. Through my choice to overcome those patterns, I prevented them from having an effect in my own life and from being passed down to my own children.

On Easter Sunday when I was in the program, we all gathered in the classroom to have a time of worship. I was not expecting a supernatural encounter with God—I just wanted to worship Him. However, when the music started, I began weeping. I could not stop crying. The Holy Spirit was truly working in my heart and I was never the same after that moment. As I cried out all of the shame, guilt, and anger that I had carried for so long; God was healing my heart. My counselor had been praying for me to have a revelation of God's love, and I believe He answered her prayer as well as my own that day at Mercy.

I know that you can feel God's love through other people, but it is difficult to have a deep understanding of His love until you have had an encounter with the Holy Spirit. The Holy Spirit does speak through people, nature, and in other ways, but when someone has an encounter with His presence, they will never be the same. You can't make a revelation happen—it happens supernaturally, but God promises that when you ask, you shall receive.

During my life, I had never experienced unconditional love. I did not even know what love was. I think all humans want to be loved from the inside out, even with their flaws, attitudes, and weaknesses.

I wanted to know I could be loved even though I made mistakes. I wanted someone to treat me as valuable and validate what I had to say. I felt unconditional love at Mercy. I was not perfect in the program, but through it all, I was loved and corrected in love. I was used to harsh punishment and abuse when being corrected, but at Mercy I received love instead. At first, I wanted to fight it because I didn't understand it, but eventually I gave up running from love, and I ran right into it. Love changed my life.

The hardest part of freedom was remembering that although God worked through Mercy to bring me healing, Mercy didn't "fix" me. After I graduated, I was shocked when I faced struggles because I thought it meant that I should go back into the program. That was not the case! Mercy provided me with the tools I needed and introduced me to a loving Father who walks with me through life's ups and downs. Failure is not being down, but failure is refusing to get back up.

Having accountability was a main reason I did not go back to the eating disorder. Amazing people in my life walked with me step by step to make sure I stayed on my road to freedom. Being in an atmosphere that encouraged me and uplifted me helped me avoid temptations. I was able to have my quiet times with God, pray, and read the Word. I did what Mercy taught me to do until it became a lifestyle.

There have been times when I have been tempted to go back to eating disorder behaviors, and I have had to call someone to actually sit with me while I ate. There have also been times where I have fallen into old sin patterns. In those moments of weakness, when I have had to call someone to pray with me or to come and just sit with me while I vented or talked about what was on my mind, the Holy Spirit has granted me grace, ease, peace, and helped me get back on the right track again.

After I graduated from Mercy, I went to the St. Louis Dream Center where I learned how to have a deeper relationship with God. There is so much more to God than simply receiving freedom—that is only the first part! His Word is alive and has so much depth. My passion is for women to understand that the Creator of the Universe loves them. I am now working in one of the Mercy Ministries' homes, and I help young women learn to love and accept themselves as He does.

—**Kacy**

# Personal Study Guide—How does this apply to my life?

1. Kacy spent years trying to meet unrealistic expectations that she felt were put on her by other people in her life. When she realized that she was unable to please those around her she felt worthless and invaluable. What have you experienced in your life that has contributed to your feelings of worthlessness and invalue?

_____

_____

_____

_____

_____

2. What does Jeremiah 31:3–17 tell you about your true worth and value?

_____

_____

_____

_____

3. Kacy spent a lot of time studying pro-ana web sites, which encourage girls in their eating disorder by offering unhealthy tips. These sites caused her to have unrealistic expectations of her own body. Can you identify the sources in your life that contribute to your desire to meet unrealistic expectations? What are some of the expectations you have held yourself to, that may be unrealistic?

_____

_____

_____

_____

_____

4. Assuming that she would only be looked at for her flaws and weaknesses, Kacy never truly understood what love was. As she began pursuing God, He gave her a revelation of His love. What does God promise in Luke 11:9?

_____

_____

_____

_____

_____

5. A Godly and realistic goal for your life is to become the person that God created you to be. What Godly characteristics do you find listed in 1 Peter 1:5–7?

_____

_____

_____

_____

_____

6. Look at each Godly characteristic that you listed and explain how you would like to see it developed in your own life.

_____

_____

_____

_____

_____

## Talk to God

Use this space to write down any prayers, thoughts, or feelings you may have. This is a place to journal how you really feel.

_____

_____

_____

_____

_____

_____

_____

_____

_____

_____

_____

_____

_____

## Scripture to Study:

"The Lord appeared to us in the past, saying: I have loved you with an everlasting love; I have drawn you with loving-kindness."
—Jeremiah 31:3

*Chapter Eight*

# HAYLEY'S STORY: OVERWHELMED WITH GUILT

*M*y mother was my source of love, comfort, and happiness throughout my childhood. Without any warning signs, my mom became very sick and was diagnosed with leukemia. I was broken inside. She was sick for what seemed like forever. At one point, the cancer went into remission and it seemed my mom had finally won the battle, but it was only a matter of time before the disease came back. When I was eight years old, my world turned upside down the day she died. I began to feel an overwhelming burden of guilt for the many things I could have done to make her life easier. I even convinced myself that I had played a part in her death.

With my mom gone, I was often left alone with my brother. We always found something to fight about. He became aggressive and made every day a living nightmare. My self-worth took a daily beating because of his verbal, emotional, and physical abuse. As a result, I started to believe some of the awful things my brother said to me. This went on for years, leaving me feeling helpless and insecure.

When I was in the seventh grade, my dad's friend came to stay with us while he was going through a divorce. He seemed like a nice guy, but was very sexually inappropriate toward me. Disgusted and frightened by his weird affection, I began to hide from him. Feeling overwhelmed with feelings of guilt and shame, I used cutting as a way to communicate the feelings I had difficulty expressing.

In addition to the self-harm, I began to exercise obsessively. There were exercise routines hanging on every wall in my bedroom. I would spend hours a day escaping reality by focusing on my physical imperfections. To compensate for feeling overweight, I started to limit what I ate to one meal a day. Eventually, I resorted to not eating anything for days at a time, while exercising and taking diet and caffeine pills to get through the day. I became increasingly aware of the amount of calories, fat, and sugar contained in every food item.

My choice of clothing also changed in an attempt to hide my body. I wore guy's pants, which were a few sizes too big, and loose t-shirts. My wardrobe not only hid my figure, but it made me feel secure in my own skin.

I had friends at school who told me that my eating habits weren't normal, but I refused to admit that I had a problem. My teachers also recognized my weight loss and the difference in my attitude that resulted from the lack of nutrition, diet pills, and over exercising. I started to randomly pass out and I lost large amounts of hair from being so malnourished. My family ignored my weight loss. They were afraid and unsure of what to do, so they did nothing.

I had been a Christian for years, but I was more devoted to losing weight and focusing on the sickness of my eating disorder than I was on developing my relationship with God. The eating disorder took all of my time and energy. At times, I actually ignored God because I thought He would make me gain weight or make it impossible to lose it. I knew He wanted what was best for me, but I wanted to be the one in control.

During my freshman year of college, I ended up in a psychiatric ward when the eating disorder and self-harm got completely out of control. During this time, I remembered hearing about Mercy Ministries and with the help of my counselor, I filled out the application.

I came to Mercy totally broken, believing I was worthless and that true healing was impossible for me. Throughout my time at Mercy, God showed me that I could trust Him. As I began to eat in a healthy, well-balanced way, God helped me stabilize my weight and feel good about my body. I began to see how distorted my perception of myself was and how many lies I had built my life upon. I learned to replace the lies I believed with His truth.

Mercy was totally different from the mental institution I had gone to, as well as the many therapists and psychiatrists I had seen. The counselors at Mercy were so personal and passionate about helping me overcome my struggles. Whenever I hit a roadblock and felt I couldn't continue, the staff refused to give up on me. They knew my potential and continually reminded me of it.

Ultimately, it was God who gave me the strength to fight the anorexia and self-harm. God showed me, through His Word, that I have a purpose and a future. He helped me see that I am beautiful and worthy of love. Now, my list of truths about God and myself seem to be endless, whereas before, they didn't even exist. The more truth I read, the more I began to see areas of my life that needed healing. I learned that one of the first steps I needed to take was to forgive.

At Mercy, I went through a process with my counselor where I made a list of people I needed to forgive. Choosing to forgive made it possible for me to open myself up and let God in. I had let bitterness and unforgiveness build up inside of me, which was hindering my relationship with God. I became aware that my healing was a process, but forgiveness was a choice. As I began forgiving those who had hurt me, it allowed me to release them and trust God. I had to give my wounded heart over to Him and let Him mend it with His love, rather than try to get revenge on my own. Forgiveness also enabled me to give up my victim mentality and walk in the authority God meant for me to have.

During the forgiveness process at Mercy, I was very open with my dad. I shared with him my decision to forgive my mom, because I felt like she had abandoned me through her death. I also forgave my brother for abusing me physically, emotionally, and mentally. This was the first time I was honest with my dad about the abuse. Learning how to forgive has helped me to have better communication with those around me.

After I graduated from Mercy, I moved back to California and my church family became my source of support. I had become accustomed to the constant supervision I'd had at Mercy, so I had to set up structure and accountability in my life. Therefore, I started meeting with a lady at my church. Accountability and support have been very significant to my continued healing. Support is very important as you walk into the new life you've worked so diligently to establish. Without that support, it would be easy to fall into temptation.

Staying committed to God and His Word has also helped me maintain my victory over the eating disorder and self-harm. I have a tendency to get lost in my thoughts, and Satan is aware of this weakness. I need to choose daily to stay in the Word of God and to constantly renew my mind. This process has not been easy, but God has seen me through it all. Secular treatment encouraged me to focus on food and my problems, but through Mercy, I learned to stay focused on God and allow Him to change me on the inside.

By focusing on God, I know that I don't carry the burden of my issues alone, and I do not have to be afraid that the process will be more than I can handle. God and I are in this together, and my strength comes from Him. The truth that comes from His Word is dependable, solid, and immovable. My foundation is now solid rather than cracked.

I am working to finish college with a major in kinesiology and a minor in counseling. God has given me a heart for ministry, and I plan to devote my life to showing young girls the hope and future that awaits them while helping them achieve victory! I never thought freedom was possible, but Christ has shown me through my own testimony that it is!

—**Hayley**

## Personal Study Guide—How does this apply to my life?

1.  Hayley developed an overwhelming burden of guilt that she carried with her, leading her to self-destructive behaviors. In what ways can you identify feelings of guilt and shame in your own life?

_____

_____

_____

_____

_____

2.  How do you react when you feel those emotions? List the effects that guilt and shame have on your behaviors.

    _____

    _____

    _____

    _____

    _____

3.  Hayley carried a lot of guilt, feeling like she caused her mother's death. Identify areas where you may be taking false responsibility by carrying guilt for something that you did not cause. Ask someone you trust to help you if you are unsure if you are taking false responsibility. Pray through each one and ask God to help you release these burdens.

    _____

    _____

    _____

    _____

    _____

4.  Guilt and shame are not from God. The truth is that Jesus, God's only Son, died on the cross and took on your guilt and shame so that you could live free from that burden. What does Isaiah 53:5 say about how Jesus' death on the cross affects you?

    _____

    _____

    _____

    _____

    _____

5. Forgiveness is a major part of the healing process. Once you have made the choice to forgive others, you have opened the door for God's forgiveness in your own life. When you find yourself overwhelmed with shame and guilt, the first person you may need to forgive is yourself. Ask God to reveal to you the things that you need to forgive yourself for and let go of, so you can move forward into your future instead of being bound by your past. Make a list of those things and then ask for God's forgiveness.

   _____

   _____

   _____

   _____

   _____

6. Forgiveness often opens the door for healing in relationships in your life. As you forgive people and release the feelings of bitterness and resentment to God, you will notice that your attitude will begin to change as well. In what relationships do you see the need for restoration, and what steps can you take today to open the doors of forgiveness and communication with those people?

   There are times when a relationship may be dangerous or unhealthy. While it is still necessary to forgive those people in your heart, direct communication may not be wise. Please talk to a mature Christian friend or counselor if you are unsure about the steps you need to take with a relationship in your life.

   _____

   _____

   _____

   _____

   _____

Take time to pray for those whom you have forgiven. Praying for others who have hurt you opens up even more healing in your life and opens the door for God to work in the lives of the people who have hurt you.

## Talk to God

Use this space to write down any prayers, thoughts, or feelings you may have. This is a place to journal how you really feel.

_____

_____

_____

_____

_____

_____

_____

_____

_____

_____

_____

_____

## Scripture to Study:

"Instead of their shame my people will receive a double portion, and instead of disgrace they will rejoice in their inheritance; and so they will inherit a double portion in their land, and everlasting joy will be theirs."

—Isaiah 61:7

# PRACTICAL WAYS TO WALK INTO FREEDOM

*W*hile the source of true healing and freedom is found only through God and His Word, there are many practical steps you need to take when overcoming an eating disorder. Freedom is a process and may not happen immediately, but as it says in Philippians 1:6, "He who began a good work in you will carry it on to completion until the day of Christ Jesus."

### *First and Foremost . . .*

It is important to establish care with a local physician in whom you can confide the details of your current struggle. It is very important that you speak honestly regarding your behaviors with this physician in order for you to receive the best care possible. Likely, you will need blood work taken to determine the current physical state of your body. Significantly restricting food or purging food on a regular basis can have a negative effect on you physically. Your physician will guide you in how to best regain balance in your body and start on the road to good health.

During the start of your restoration period, it is important to begin supplementing your diet with a multi-vitamin because your body is depleted of the vitamins and minerals that it needs. A calcium supplement will also greatly benefit you because of the probable loss of bone density that has occurred as a result of the eating disorder. Ultimately, your physician will be able to direct you as to what you are specifically in need of after assessing your situation.

### *Food and Nutrition*

As you are walking out of the bondage of an eating disorder, it is important to make healthy food choices, eat healthy portions, as well as balance the inclusion of sweets. Your body requires a variety of foods to be able to perform the proper functions each day. The major nutrient categories include: carbohydrates, healthy fat, fiber, protein, vitamins, minerals, and water. Each nutrient does something specific in the body, thus allowing you to maintain the health you need to move through life. You can find food sources of each of the nutrient categories by observing the Food Pyramid. This guide provides standard food groups for our daily food needs.

If you battle with anorexia you may be reducing or even omitting one or more food groups. If this is where you are, begin to include a small portion of food (about the size of your palm) from each of the nutrient groups. Start by eating small meals throughout the day, focusing especially on breakfast. Once you are able to eat three small meals, you can move into healthy snacks, especially if you need to restore your body to a healthy weight range.

If you battle bulimia, you may tend to over-eat a particular food or food group (often carbohydrates and/or sweets) and then purge the food back up. Binge-eating is similar to bulimia with the exception of purging. In either situation, start by eating healthy portions in each nutrient group and allow for a serving of sweets occasionally, so you're not tempted to over-eat due to deprivation.

Another tool for getting these behaviors under control is accountability. Identify a supportive individual that you will allow to ask you regularly if you are engaging in any eating disorder behaviors. You may want to place yourself for an hour or so away from a bathroom after each meal to make purging more difficult. Another accountability tool is to keep a food journal of everything you eat and drink in a day, and share it with your accountability person for support. When you are sharing your struggles with another person, often you will be more conscious of making the right choice in the moment of temptation.

## *Physical Fitness*

When it comes to physical fitness and physical wellness, you have to learn about your body again. How does it move? What are certain movements supposed to feel like? Why do certain positions cause more pain than others? The answers to these questions can be found by starting a physical fitness regimen that will help to undo the past damage from your eating disorder, while restoring your body to the design that God originally intended. It is possible, and a physical fitness routine could help.

Prior to starting a fitness regimen of any kind, it is imperative that you are consuming an adequate amount of water each day. The general guideline for daily water intake is 64 fluid ounces or 8 cups. Water is a crucial element for your body's restoration.

When starting any kind of physical fitness routine, the most important thing to remember is to start slowly and limit your workouts to a few times per week by doing rehabilitation and functional movement exercises, muscle toning exercises, beginner or intermediate level Pilates or Yoga. These types of workouts will start to not only build a new foundation, but they will also help your body to restore itself in the area of strength, flexibility, and muscular endurance. Once this foundation has been laid, it will be important for you to take small steps towards slowly increasing the sets and/or repetitions that you are doing without necessarily taking more time or adding more days. Also, it is extremely important for you to limit your amount of cardiovascular exercise (i.e.: walking, jogging, hiking, etc) until your body is at a more stable place and can withstand medium intensity workouts without any dizziness, light-headedness, or excessive fatigue.

Compulsive exercise is commonly used by girls who are struggling with an eating disorder as a way to control their weight and create a calorie deficit. Suggested ways to combat this type of eating disorder behavior are to have accountability when it comes to how long you are at the gym and to chart your weekly progress. This includes the types of exercises that you do as well as setting small goals for the upcoming week. An example of accountability could be taking a friend with you to a group fitness class at your local gym and limiting your exercise to only include that class.

Although the amount and frequency of your physical fitness regimen is going to vary depending on the severity of the eating disorder, the principles are the same for all types of eating disorders.

# ABOUT MERCY MINISTRIES

*M*ercy Ministries exists to provide opportunities for young women to experience God's unconditional love, forgiveness, and life-transforming power. We provide residential programs free of charge to young women ages 13–28 who are dealing with life-controlling issues such as eating disorders, self-harm, addictions, sexual abuse, unplanned pregnancy, and depression. Our approach addresses the underlying roots of these issues by addressing the whole person—spiritually, physically, and emotionally—and produces more than just changed behavior; the Mercy Ministries program changes hearts and stops destructive cycles.

Founded in 1983 by Nancy Alcorn, Mercy Ministries currently operates in three states and in Australia, Canada, New Zealand, and the UK, with plans for additional US and international locations underway. We are blessed to have connecting relationships with many different Christian congregations, but are not affiliated with any church, organization, or denomination. Residents enter Mercy Ministries on a voluntary basis and stay an average of six months. Our program includes life-skills training and educational opportunities that help ensure the success of our graduates. Our goal is for each young woman to not only complete the program, but also to discover the purpose for her life and bring value to her community as a productive citizen.

## BEYOND STARVED

For more information, visit our Web site at
www.mercyministries.com.

**Mercy Ministries of America**
www.mercyministries.com

**Mercy Ministries Australia**
www.mercyministries.com.au

**Mercy Ministries Canada**
www.mercycanada.com

**Mercy Ministries UK**
www.mercyministries.co.uk

**Mercy Ministries New Zealand**
www.mercyministries.org.nz

**Mercy Ministries Peru**
www.mercyministries.com

# ABOUT THE AUTHOR

*D*uring and after college, Nancy Alcorn, a native Tennessean, spent eight years working for the state of Tennessee at a correctional facility for juvenile delinquent girls and investigating child abuse cases. Working for the state allowed her to experience firsthand the secular programs, which were not producing permanent results exemplified by changed lives. Nancy saw many of the girls pass the age of eighteen and end up in the women's prison system because they never got the real help they needed. She knew lasting change would never come as the result of any government system.

After working for the state, she was appointed Director of Women for Nashville Teen Challenge, where she worked for two years. Through her experience, she came to realize that only Jesus could bring restoration into the lives of these girls who were deeply hurting and desperately searching for something to fill the void they felt in their hearts. She knew God was revealing a destiny that would result in her stepping out to do something to help young women.

In January 1983, determined to establish a program in which lives would truly be transformed, Nancy moved to Monroe, Louisiana, to start Mercy Ministries of America. God instructed Nancy to do three specific things to ensure His blessings on the ministry: (1) not to take any state or federal funding that might limit the freedom to teach Christian principles, (2) to accept girls free of charge, and (3) to always give at least 10 percent of all Mercy Ministries' donations to other Christian organizations and ministries. As Nancy has continued to be faithful to these three principles, God has been faithful to provide for every need of the ministry just as He promised.

In Monroe, Nancy began with a small facility for troubled girls. After adding on twice to make additional space in the original home, Nancy began to see the need for an additional home to meet the special needs of unwed mothers. For this dream to be realized on a debt-free basis, Nancy knew she would need to raise funds. No doubt, God knew the need and already had a plan in place.

One day, Nancy, exhausted from speaking at an evangelism conference in Las Vegas, boarded a plane for home. The man sitting next to her seemed ready for a chat. When he asked her how much money she had lost gambling, Nancy told him she hadn't gone to Vegas to gamble and shared briefly about Mercy Ministries with him. He seemed interested, so Nancy gave him a brochure as they parted. About four weeks later, this same man called Nancy to ask her for more details about Mercy Ministries and said he felt compelled to help in some way. It was then that Nancy told him about the plans for the unwed mothers' home. He told her he had been adopted when he was five days old. His heart was so touched that he wrote a check to Mercy Ministries for the exact amount needed to help build the second Mercy Ministries house debt-free.

You can read Nancy's entire story in her book *Echoes of Mercy*.

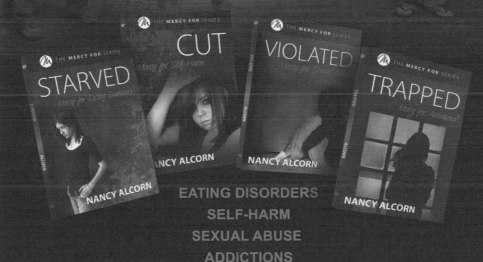